ESSAYS IN METAPHYSICS:
IDENTITY AND DIFFERENCE

MARTIN HEIDEGGER

Essays
in Metaphysics:
Identity and Difference

PHILOSOPHICAL LIBRARY INC.
New York

Translated from the German *Identität und Differenz*
by Kurt F. Leidecker.

Printed in the United States of America

TABLE OF CONTENTS

ESSAYS IN METAPHYSICS:

IDENTITY AND DIFFERENCE

INTRODUCTION

There is scarce need to comment on the importance of the two lectures translated here which were published in 1957 under the title of *Identität und Differenz*. In them Heidegger does not go into all the ramifications of his philosophy, and they do not answer all questions of Heidegger's existentialism. Yet, even in the casual reader the impression must surely be created that here we have the ruminations of a master mind in his maturity. The sensitive and attentive reader will come away with a feeling that he now knows Heidegger, the man, the teacher, better. He will receive illuminating insights into Heidegger's thinking on many a vital issue, our technological age, religion, language, history, for on all of which subjects and more besides he has touched upon here, if only epigrammatically.

Through these lectures Heidegger enables us even better to assign him a place as one of the leading figures in the history of philosophy. Always conscious of the tremendous contributions of western thinking, he seems more concise in his hints at a *confirmatio* and *lux ex Oriente*. There is no ranting against anything, which has of late become the royal sport and pastime of many professing the love of wisdom. There is no anxiety, no fear, no gloom here which settles like fallout on us when reading some of the existentialists and would-be existentialists. There is not a word of fretting, testiness and peevishness which might even be pardonable. You say the theme did not warrant it? Of course, it never does, yet how many disciples of the royal science pay attention to the warranty?

Here is wisdom charmingly, lumberingly expressed, with a little interlarding of a fairy tale, some brightly illuminating passages, such as Kant also gave us, a skating on the thin ice of etymology, quaint excursions into language not heard for decades or even centuries, a quiet acceptance of what the ground swells of Being have in store for us.

Heidegger would be difficult to understand if we did not know Plato, Parmenides, Leibniz, Spinoza, Kant, and particularly Hegel, those great landmarks on the march of idealism. Yet knowledge is not enough. As if acknowledging an ancient eastern tradition, Heidegger goes to the womb of things, beyond language to the home of speech to draw the final inspiration. Even more marvelous than that, and possibly unknown to the master himself, his very choice of words is reminiscent in the under- and overtones of such quaint words as *Gestell, Gesetz, Gepräge, Satz,* and *wesen,* of an ancient and universal symbolism which certainly gives a new slant on Heidegger's own power of penetrating uncommonly deeply.

2

Heidegger passionately seeks Being, but he seeks it through Existence, in Existence, and pursues it relentlessly to the essence of both. His logic dissolves into ontology, both into theology, and all in the Logos, the Ground. There is fluidity; his whole thought structure floats lightly on evanescent clouds of thought like those heavenly palaces in Buddhist legends, but he bids us wing ourselves in spirit up to them and waft through Being and Existence.

His allusion to forgetfulness, though based on the Greek concept, blends into the oriental nescience, while the "object of thought" makes perfect analogy to *vidyā*, which is knowledge without superciliousness, without "externality." One often feels that Heidegger says in "one of our western languages" what has been not-said, yet loudly and openly proclaimed in Zen.

Far from making Heidegger out to be a mystic, his endeavor to get at Being and essence is metempiric. Weaponed with the keenest of tools of absolute idealism, combined with those of semantics, he explores the involvement of man in the whole of Being, realizing full well that all these tools must be discarded or transformed. The problem is how to see the eye that sees, not the eye that is reflected. It is, indeed, the age-old quest, *the* basic quest of all philosophy of all the ages. Heidegger knows he is not the first and he will not be the last to intellectually penetrate the essence. But he is the most intelligible, though he is obscure himself on occasion and his disciples even feel at times that communication is breaking off.

What makes Heidegger important is his receptiveness, his sensitivity, his ability to lie at the heart of the problem and "see" and "hear" when others see and hear nothing. That is why others leap, if at all they dare, in fear and trembling before an abyss into which he, like the *śūnyavādin* of Buddhist philosophy throws himself happily, though it spells emptiness and nothingness to others, to discover in it womb what the whole of actual existence is not and has not, —the totality of which is stupendous.

Yes, the problem is one of identity and difference, and we have been blind so long because we read words, as Parmenides' about the Same, but treat them, at best, with a paternalistic air as archaic. Now, at last, we understand identity, because we must seek it at the source. Difference also is clarified and its edge dulled. Metaphysics, we find, in the West was but a halfhearted attempt because we did not know how to penetrate to the essence, though we know it to be there. Heidegger makes us at home where we have been putting up so long uncomfortably and with want of grace and gratitude.

The interesting part of Heidegger's philosophy is that we do not have to "get rid of," "shed," and repudiate any of our stupid or sage notions of which we are so proud in western history. We should never forget that we are part of Being, we are its very unfoldment. Call it destiny, but if you call it that remember you are destiny also by virtue of participation in Being. Look within.

By the same token look without if your world of technology threatens to engulf you and you call on scientists, politicians and humanitarians to pull you back from the brink. This cry to be saved, to do something before it is too late, to make undone what has been done, is the cry of immature beings who willfully made themselves strangers at home.

Similarly with God. God is in human civilization,— man says so, man behaves accordingly. There are innumerable religions with and without theology. But theology has become a stereotyped, lifeless endeavor. It lacks gravity in every sense of the word, it forgets its deep anchorage in the *logia*. Externalization here also instead of firming in the *Logos*. In *that* ground meet science, religion, philosophy. The Ultimate, the One is in every *logion* and *sophia* as the motivating, explaining, self-revealing reality. God for Heidegger is not the god of images and of worships, he is the strength of piety, he is that which moves and in whose self-caused Being those who are attuned find rational, universal support. Heidegger's God dissolves as entity, yet electrifies the Whole as divinity.

The old metaphysics is done, so are old-style ontology and theology. The progress they made was a retreat from the ground of it all. Now we have to turn about and make our way back, backtrack as it were. Heidegger preaches no doom, he is neither dogmatic nor categorical. He presents us with the supremely logical which is not exhausted in a formal exercise but follows through to the essence, sounding, probing, listening.

The trials and tribulations of this voyage toward essence are reflected in the linguistic expression which, naturally, concerns the translator in more than one way. He could easily have tagged his translation a tentative one—for the original is, admittedly, difficult—and thus escape much of the responsibility for what may not be too felicitous in English. He could also have made a "free" translation and liberally indulged in paraphrase. The result might have made any "trained rapid reader who nevertheless comprehends fully what he reads" happy. In doing the translation as literally as permissible (how much this word is abused by critics, since it is usually an unanswerable charge, and by others who confuse literal with word-for-word and general unintelligibility), yet, it is hoped, without contorting the English language, several purposes were in the translator's mind which he thought would be worth-while to achieve.

First of all there is the student of philosophy who may, as he should, be persuaded that language adds an almost evanescent something to thought which, if anywhere, especially in existentialism ought to be caught. For him it would be easier to compare or check the translation if it did not stray vocabulary- and syntax-wise too far from the original.

Again, it seems incongruous to put too freely what requires the rigor of logic itself and bears neither embellishment nor extension nor contraction. We may be dealing with God, "existence" and the like, but it must be remembered that in Heidegger theology becomes theo*logic* and ontology becomes onto*logic*, just as in the German idealistic tradition they speak of a *science* of logic and a doctrine of science which far transcends what we take science to be.

And, finally, much of what Heidegger speculates about is interlaced with seeming alliterations and actual etymologies. It near requires philological training to follow him into Greek and Latin, Old German, Middle High German and cognate languages. How much latitude could one permit oneself in "translating freely" when the context actually begs to parallel the German in the English? Thus, hours were spent in "listening" to the susurrations of a certain word beyond what it announces in discourse, esoterically, as it were. It was not possible in every case to find an English etymologically sound parallel, nor a semantically correct equivalent. Discovering "to fathom" for *ergründen* was, of course, very easy, for like the German it means "getting to the bottom" in a literal as well as figurative sense. But we were, for instance, not quite so lucky in *begründen* and feel we should apologize for "to under stand," having the flimsy excuse that the components of the English word would seem to establish a certain kinship with the German. Yet, when "confronted" (in a very real sense!) with variations upon the *Grund*, such as *gründen, im Grunde, von Grund aus,* and *im grün-*

denden Grunde, we frankly were stymied many a time though never forgetful that Heidegger takes these as variations upon "basis," "foundation," "reason," "cause" and Logos all at once. Here is where the more literal translation may be of greater service in aiding the student in eventually hitting upon a lucky translation rather than guessing at the meaning. He may even be less frustrated than when "confronted" by a flowery translation with the German word in parenthesis which leaves him breathless and perhaps dazed.

One final thought which may be superfluous for those who read. If Heidegger was one of the first of modern existentialists and the teacher of a Sartre among others, how much have existentialists strayed and been trapped in dark alleys? And if Heidegger's thinking really is, as we think it is, the consummation of a long tradition in western metaphysics and meta-ontology, how much is what he teaches like the intuitive, sometimes dramatically paradoxical teaching of the East, thus closing a mighty circle?

KURT F. LEIDECKER

*Mary Washington College
of the University of Virginia*

PREFACE

The chapter entitled "The Principle of Identity" represents the unchanged text of a lecture given the 27th of June, 1957. The occasion was the Day of Faculties at the celebration of the 500th year of the founding of the University of Freiburg in the Breisgau, Germany.

The chapter on "The Onto-theo-logical Nature of Metaphysics" is the partly revised investigation which formed the conclusion of a seminar on Hegel's Science of Logic which was held during the winter semester of 1956-57. The lecture was given in Todtnauberg on the 24th of February, 1957.

In "The Principle of Identity" we are offering backward and forward glances. The chapter points ahead into the realm which forms the basis of the discussion for the lecture on "The Thing." [1] It refers back to the realm in which the essence of metaphysics takes its rise, metaphysics whose nature is characterized by *difference*.

The togetherness of *identity* and *difference* will be demonstrated in the present publication as the object of thought.

In how far difference has its origin in the nature of identity the reader may discover for himself when he is attentive to the harmony prevailing between event[2] and issue.[3]

Nothing in this sphere it is possible to prove, but much can be hinted.

Todtnauberg,
September 9th, 1957

The Principle of Identity

THE PRINCIPLE OF IDENTITY

The principle of identity is expressed by the common formula $A=A$. This principle is looked upon as the first law of thought. We shall endeavor to reflect a little on this principle, for by it we would like to find out what is meant by identity.

Should our thinking, after having been stimulated by something or other, pursue this certain thing it might happen that the thing will change in the process. Hence it is advisable to pay close attention to the method employed, and less so to the content. Obviously, we are also prevented from dwelling too much on the content, since we are under obligation to get on with this lecture.

What does the formula $A=A$, by which we customarily express the principle of identity, state? The formula states that A and A are equal. Now, for something to be equal we must have at least two items. One A is equal to another. Is this really what the principle of identity intends to express? Apparently not. The identical, in Latin *idem*, is called in Greek *to autó*. Translated into the German language *to autó* is called *das Selbe*, the Same. If someone should keep on stating the same, let us say, "the plant is a plant," he would speak tautologically. In order for anything to be the same, however, only one of its kind is required at any one time, and not two, as would be the case with equality.

The formula $A = A$ deals, however, with equality. It does not designate A as the same. Hence, the well-known formulation of the principle of identity conceals precisely what the principle endeavors to state, which is, that A is A, or every A is itself the Same.

In rendering the identical thus, we are reminded of an old phrase in which Plato is driving home what he means by something identical, a phrase which goes back to a still earlier one. In the dialogue *Sophist 254d* Plato is speaking of *stásis* and *kínesis*, of arrested motion and sudden reversal. In this passage Plato has the stranger say: *Oukoun autōn hékaston toîn men duoîn héterón estin, auto d'heautō tautón.* "Now, each of the two, let us be sure, is another, while each is with respect to itself the same." Plato is not merely saying *hékaston autō tautón*, "every self the same," but *hékaston heautō tautón*, "each with respect to itself the same."

The dative *heauto* signifies that each, which is itself, has been returned upon itself; each which is itself, is the same, meaning, for itself unto itself. The German language sacrifices[4] in this case, in a like manner as does the Greek, the advantage of making clear what is meant by the identical, but it does so, as it were, in a fugue of a number of variations.

14

The more adequate formula for the principle of identity A is A states, therefore, not only that every A as such is the same. Rather, it states that every A as such is the same with respect to itself. In the state of being oneself there is embodied the relationship "with." Thus we have a mediation, a connection, a synthesis: a unification into a oneness. It is owing to this circumstance that throughout the history of occidental thinking identity appears with the character of unity. Nevertheless, this unity is by no means the jejune emptiness of what, in the absence of internal relations, remains in persisting monotony. However, western thought needed more than 2000 years before this relation with itself (which is present in identity and was hinted already at an early date) appeared definitely and well developed as a process of mediation, before, moreover, men's minds became hospitable to the idea of a manifestation of a mediation within identity. It was not until the philosophy of speculative idealism made its appearance in Fichte, Schelling and Hegel, after Leibniz and Kant had prepared the way, that the concept of identity, whose nature consists in synthesis, met with receptivity. We cannot go into details here. Only one thing must be borne in mind. Ever since the era of speculative idealism we are no longer permitted to think of the unity of identity as a monotonous sameness, or neglect to recognize the mediation prevailing in unity. In the contrary event we would be taking identity as merely abstract.

Even in the improved formula "A is A" only the abstractness of identity is apparent. Is this actually what we shall end up with? Doesn't the principle of identity say anything about identity? No, at least not immediately. Rather, the principle presupposes what we call identity and to what category it belongs. And how do we get to know concerning this presupposition? The principle of identity is furnishing us the information, provided we listen carefully to its keynote and ponder over it instead of merely reciting the formula "A is A" in a superficial manner. Actually, the formula should be intoned A *is* A. And what do we hear then? Through the "is" the principle conveys the mode of existence of every Existent, to the effect that as such it is the same with itself. The principle of identity expresses something about the Being of Existence. As a law of thought the principle is valid only in so far as it is a law of Being which states: To every Existent as such belongs identity, the oneness with itself.

What the principle of identity proclaims as we are listening to its keynote is precisely what the whole of western European thinking thinks: Unity of identity is a characteristic feature in the Being of Existence. No matter where and how we face an Existent, identity makes a claim upon us. Should there be no claim, the Existent would never be able to appear in its Being. Accordingly, there would also be no science. For science could not be what it is if the self-identity of its object, whatever it may be, were not guaranteed

at the outset. By virtue of this warranty the possibility of scientific enquiry is assured. Nevertheless,
this dominant conception of the identity of the object
is of no tangible avail to science, and as a result the
success and fruitfulness of scientific knowledge in
general are based on something useless. The claim
of the object's identity *proclaims* itself no matter
whether the sciences are perceptive of this claim or
not, whether they pay attention to what they perceive
or are befuddled by it.

The claim of identity issues from the Being of
Existence. But wherever, in occidental thinking, the
Being of Existence has been discussed rather early
and in detail, as was the case in Parmenides, the *to
autó*, the identical, gives forth with almost boundless
scope. One of Parmenides' sayings runs as follows:
to gar auto noeîn estin te kai eînai, "the Same is, to
wit, Perceiving (Thinking) as well as Being." [5]

Thinking and Being, two disparates, are here
thought of as the Same. What is the meaning of this?
If we compare what we otherwise recognize as the
teaching of metaphysics, something vastly different
from identity belonging to Being is announced here.
Parmenides says: Being inheres in identity. What,
then, is meant here by identity? What is conveyed
by the word *to autó*, the Same, in Parmenides' saying?

Parmenides does not provide us with an answer to
this question. He confronts us with a puzzle, a puzzle
we ought not try to circumvent. It is incumbent on

17

us to recognize the following. In the prime of thought, and long before the principle of identity was expressed, identity asserted itself and, to be sure, in an aphorism which decrees: Thinking and Being together belong to the Same, and together they stem from the Same.

Quite inadvertently we just now interpreted *to autó*, the Same. We have explained the sameness as belonging-togetherness. It is, of course, natural to visualize this belonging-together in the sense of the subsequent idea of identity with which we are in general familiar. And what would prevent us from doing just that? Nothing less than the sentence itself as we read it in Parmenides. For it states something different, to wit: Being belongs—together with Thought—to the Same. Out of an identity Being is defined as a character of this identity. Contrariwise, the identity which later on plays a rôle in metaphysical thinking is visualized as a character of Being. Thus, we cannot determine the nature of the identity of which Parmenides spoke on the basis of this metaphysically conceived identity.

The sameness of Thinking and Being as proclaimed in the words of Parmenides has a longer history behind it than the identity which metaphysics derived from a character of Being.

The main concept in the saying of Parmenides, *to autó*, the Same, remains obscure. We let it remain obscure. At the same time, we are open to suggestions emanating from the statement at the opening of which we find it.

18

In the meantime, however, it seems we have already settled the sameness of Thinking and Being in the belonging-together of both. This was a hasty move. Possibly it was forced upon us. Now it is incumbent on us to cancel what we so rashly maintained. We can do it, of course, in that we are not taking the above-mentioned belonging-together as the final or even sole authoritative interpretation of the sameness of Thinking and Being.

If we think of belonging-*together* in the accustomed manner, then the meaning of what we discern—as indicated by the stress within the word—is determined by the togetherness, that is, its unity. In this case "to belong" is equivalent to being coordinated with and incorporated into the order of togetherness, ranged into the oneness of a manifold, or placed into a structural unity of a system with the help of the unifying core of an appropriate synthesis. This belonging-togetherness is presented in philosophy as a *nexus* or *connexio,* as the necessary combination of one thing with another.

Nevertheless, belonging-together may also be thought of as a *belonging*-together. In other words, togetherness is now determined by belongingness. In this case, however, we are obliged to enquire what the meaning of "belonging" is and how the character of togetherness may be determined in it. The answer to this question is closer to our minds than we might think at first; nevertheless it is not obvious. It may suffice for the present if our attention is, thus, directed to the possibility of visualizing belonging as no longer derived from the unity of togetherness, but to the possibility of learning about being together through belonging. However, the question may be asked, whether this suggested possibility is nothing more than a mere play upon words which conjures up something lacking all support in a verifiable situation?

This is, indeed, the situation as it appears until we take a closer look and allow the problem to develop naturally.

The idea of belonging-together, in the sense of a *belonging* together, originated in view of a situation already alluded to. To be sure, it is difficult to keep our attention centered on it because of the simplicity of the situation. Nevertheless, the facts will immediately strike us as more familiar if we take the following into consideration. When we were discussing belonging-together as a *belonging*-together we already had in mind, thanks to Parmenides' suggestion, Thinking as well as Being, hence what belongs together in the Same.

If we take thinking as the distinctive feature of man, then we are reminded of a *belonging*-together so far as man and Being are concerned. At that instant, however, we feel questions crowd in upon us, such as: What do we mean by Being? Who or what is Man? Everyone will easily comprehend that without a satisfactory answer to these questions we lack the foundation on which we might discover something reliable concerning the *belonging*-together of

Man and Being. However, as soon as we put the question in this manner we are fated in our attempt to visualize the togetherness of Man and Being as a co-ordination and to dispose and explain it by starting either with Man or with Being. In such a venture the traditional concepts of Man and Being furnish us with the points of anchorage for the coordination of both.

How would it be, then, if, for the purpose of establishing the unity of Man and Being we were to see whether and in what manner there is primarily a belonging-of-one-to-another involved in this togetherness, instead of stubbornly visualizing only their coordination? Why, we may even reckon with the possibility of perceiving, howbeit only from afar off, the belonging together of Man and Being right in the traditional definitions of their essence. But how can that be?

Obviously, Man represents some Existent. As such he belongs with the stone, the tree, and the eagle to the totality of Being. To belong is in this context still equivalent to being incorporated into Being. But the distinct feature of Man consists in that he, as that thinking being which is receptive to Being, is confronted by Being, remains oriented to Being and thus corresponds to Being. Man in reality *is* this reference to correspondence, and that is *all* he is. By this last phrase we do not imply limitation, but superabundance. Belonging to Being is the controlling factor of Man from within. Now, this belonging is oriented to Being because it is allocated[6] to it.

And what is Being? Let us think of Being in its original sense as presence. Man is neither casually nor exceptionally confronted by Being. Being becomes evident and lasts only so long as by virtue of its claim it draws near to Man.[7] For it is Man alone who has made himself accessible to Being, who permits Being to approach him with its presence. Such being present[8] requires the open space of a clearing and thus remains allocated to the human being by virtue of this need. This does not at all mean, however, that Being is to be posited first and only by Man. On the contrary, the following may now become clearer to our minds.

Man and Being are allocated to each other. They belong to each other. It was owing in the first place to this belonging-together (to which thinkers have not paid much attention) that Man and Being have acquired those determinations in essence by which they are comprehended metaphysically in philosophy.

This predominant *belonging*-together of Man and Being we fail to acknowledge stubbornly so long as we are looking upon everything in orderly arrangement and mediation, be it dialectically or without dialectics. In such situations we then find regularly nothing but connections which have been brought about either on the part of Being or on the part of Man and represent the belonging-together of Man and Being as an intertwining of the two.

Thus far we have not entered into[9] *belonging-*

together. The question may be asked how such homing[10] may be accomplished. The answer is by keeping aloof from the attitude of representational thinking. This keeping aloof[11] is a positing in the sense of a leap.[12] It is a bounding away from and a leaving behind of the familiar concept of Man as the *animal rationale*, the rational animal, who nowadays has become the subject for his objects. The bounding off is at the same time a getting away from Being. However, beginning early in occidental thinking, this Being has been interpreted as the ground[13] in which every Existent, as Existent, has its authentication.[14]

In what direction does the leap from the ground point? Is it heading for an abyss? It does so, indeed, so long as we picture ourselves the leap and do so more specifically within the scope of metaphysical thought. It does not head for an abyss in so far as we leap and let ourselves go. In what direction? We are going to where we are already imbedded,[15] into the fold of Being. Yet, Being itself is our very own, for only in Man can Being be domiciled, that is to say, can it *be* present.[16]

Hence we must leap in order that we may experience in our own person the *belonging*-together of Man and Being. This leap is the precipitous homing without benefit of bridges into that belongingness which alone Man and Being as mutually related and, hence, their pattern[17] can provide. The leap is the sudden return into the realm where Man and Being

23

have already found together in their essence, because both were assigned to each other in a sufficiency. It is not until the entry into the sphere of this mutual assignation is effected that thought experience becomes attuned to it and determined.

How odd this leap which we expect will provide us with the realization that we have not made ourselves sufficiently at home where, in reality, we actually already are at home. But where *are* we? What is the pattern of Being and Man?

Today we no longer need the elaborate hints still required years ago to direct our gaze to a certain pattern in which Man and Being concern each other, —at least so it seems. One might venture the opinion that it would suffice mentioning the word atomic age in order to convey how nowadays Being con-fronts us in the world of technology. However, are we entitled, without further ado, to equate the world of technical science and Being? Obviously not. Even then we should not do so when we picture ourselves the world as a whole in which atomic energy, the planned calculations of human beings, and automatization are combined. Why is it that such a reference, however detailed, to the world of technology does not, nevertheless, by any means bring the patterns of Being and Man into focus? Because every thinking analysis of the situation falls short in so far as the above-mentioned whole of the world of technology has already been prejudged in the human perspective as the product of man. Technology, in the broadest

24

sense and thought of in the manifoldness of its phe-nomena,[18] is looked upon as a man-made plan which eventually forces the human being into a decision as to whether he wishes to become slave of his plan or retain mastership over it.

In this conception of the entire world of technology we trace everything back to man and finally demand an ethics suitable to the world of technology if, in-deed, we wish to carry things that far. Caught up in this conception we then personally firm ourselves in the opinion that technology is the concern of Man alone and fail to notice the claim which Being makes on us through the very nature of technology.

Let us at long last be done with thinking about technology only technologically, that is, in terms of man and his machine. Let us pay close attention to the claim under which, in our age, not only Man but all Existence, nature and history, operate with respect to their own Being.

What claims are we referring to? Our whole exist-ence is challenged everywhere—now as in play, now urgently; now as if set upon, now as if pushed—to plan and calculate everything. What does this chal-lenge mean? Is it merely the product of man's self-generated mood? Or are we actually concerned with Existence itself in the sense that it makes a claim upon us with respect to its schematization and calculabil-ity? If such were the case, would not Being itself be then subject to the challenge of having Existence ap-pear within the purview of calculability? Such is, indeed, the case. More than that. To the extent that Being is challenged, Man is likewise challenged, that is to say, Man is "framed" so he will safeguard the Existence which concerns him as the very substance of his planning and calculating, and thus pursue this task into the immeasurable.

The term we choose for the totality of challenges which confront Man and Being mutually so they may call each other to account reciprocally, is the frame-work.[19] Some have objected to the use of this word. But are we not using instead of "to frame"[20] also to set or posit? Then we find nothing wrong in the use of the word "statute."[21] Why should we, then, not use frame-work when insight into the situation demands it?

That wherein and wherefrom Man and Being con-cern[22] each other in the world of technology, puts forth its claim much in the manner in which forces counterbalance in a frame-work.[23] In the reciprocal confrontation of Man and Being we become attentive to[24] the claim which fixes the pattern for our age. Everywhere the frame-work concerns us immediately. The frame-work—if we are still permitted to use this term—has a more pregnant existence than all atomic energies and all mechanical contrivances, a more meaningful existence than the impact of organization, information and automatization. In as much as we no longer meet what is called frame-work within the scope of ideation which allows us to think the Being of an Existent as a presence, it seems at first somewhat

26

strange. The frame-work concerns us no more than anything that is present. The frame-work remains strange most of all because it is not an ultimate but merely leads us gently to *That* which in reality pervades the pattern of Being and Man.

The *belonging*-together of Man and Being in the manner of a reciprocal challenge drives home alarmingly the that and the how of Man's alienation from Being, at the same time, however, also the that and how of Being. Within the frame-work there prevails a strange alienation[25] and dedication.[26] Now, we are under obligation to experience in our own person quite simply this concinnity wherein Man and Being are con-cinnate. In other words, we must return to what we call a *concern*.[27] The word *Ereignis* (concern) has been lifted from organically developing language. *Er-eignen* (to con-cern) means, originally, to distinguish or discern with one's eyes, see, and in seeing calling to oneself, ap-propriate. The word con-cern we shall now harness as a theme word in the service of thought, keeping in mind what has just been explained. As a theme word thus understood it may be translated with as little success as the Greek theme word *lógos* and the Chinese *Tao*. In the present context the word concern no longer signifies what we otherwise call an affair or happening.[28] We now use the word *singulare tantum*, in the singular merely. What it designates takes place only in the singular, nay, not even any longer numerically speaking, but uniquely. What we learn by way of the modern world

27

of technology in the frame-work as a pattern of Being and Man, is merely *prelude* to what we call con-cern. Con-cern, however, does not necessarily persevere in its prelude. For in con-cern we are persuaded of the possibility of developing the mere sway of the frame-work into a more primitive solicitude. Such a development of the frame-work from concern to solicitude would bring about the eventful reduction (never initiated by Man himself alone) of the world of technology from lordship to servitude within the realm in which man more properly involves himself in con-cern.

Where has our road taken us? It has led our thinking back home into that simplicity which we have called con-cern, keeping strictly to the meaning of the word. It seems as if we were now running danger of turning our thought all too insouciantly toward some generality. In actuality, however, the nearest of the near is entreating us to share immediately what we are already domiciled in. In fact, that was what we wanted to express by the word con-cern. For, what could we consider more intimate than what brings us closer to where we belong, wherein we are corporate members, that is, con-cern?

Con-cern is the internally oscillating realm through which Man and Being touch each other in their essence and attain their essential nature by divesting themselves of these determinations which metaphysics imputed to them.

To think of concern as con-cern means constructively cooperating in this internally oscillating realm. The building material for this self-supporting structure is derived by thought from speech. For, speech is the most delicate, but also the most fitful all-suppressive vibration in the floating structure of concern. In so far as our being has alienated itself in speech, concern will be our dwelling place.

We are now approaching a point in our discussion where the indelicate yet unavoidable question is forced upon us: What has concern to do with identity? The answer is: Nothing. By contrast, identity has much, if not everything to do with concern. How so? We shall answer by retracing our steps briefly.

In concern Man and Being are alienated in their essential togetherness. A first uneasy flashing of concern is glimpsed in the frame-work. This frame-work constitutes the essence of the modern world of technology. In the frame-work we catch sight of a *belonging*-together of Man and Being, wherein causative belonging alone determines the kind of togetherness and its unity. As introduction to the problem of belonging-together, in which we gave belongingness preference over togetherness, we took the saying of Parmenides: "The Same is, to wit, Thinking as well as Being." The enquiry into the meaning of the Same is the enquiry into the essence of identity. In metaphysical doctrine identity is presented as a basic character in Being. But now it turns out that Being belongs together with Thought into an identity whose essence derives from that causative belonging-together which we call concern. The essence of identity is a property of con-cern.

Provided there is something to the attempt of pointing our thinking to the original seat of the essence of identity, in what light would the title of this lecture appear? The meaning of the title "The Principle of Identity" would have undergone a change.

The principle first presents itself in the form of an axiom which presupposes identity as a trait of Being, i.e., in the ground of Existence. In the course of our discussion this principle, in the sense of a declaration, has become an "advance," [29] in the sense of a forward leap. The leap starts in Being as the ground of Existence and heads for the abyss. Nevertheless, this abyss is neither an empty nothing, nor is it a dark confusion. Rather, it is con-cern. In con-cern we get the essential vibration of what is communicated as Speech, Speech which at one time was called the home of Being. And the principle of identity now proclaims a leap required in the nature of identity and necessary if otherwise the *belonging* together of Man and Being is to penetrate to the essential luminosity of concern.

In passing from the principle as statement about identity to the "advance" in the shape of a leap into the original nature of identity, thought underwent a change. Hence facing the present squarely, it gets a glimpse—beyond the human situation—of the pattern of Being and Man in what is befitting both, that is, con-cern.

Let us assume we were faced with the expectant possibility of the frame-work (i.e., the reciprocal challenge of Man and Being to compute the calculable) entreating us in concern through which alone Man and Being attain their true nature through alienation. In that event, a way would be opened for man to experience more genuinely the totality of the modern world of technology, nature and history, but above all their Being.

As long as we contemplate the world of the atomic age in all seriousness and with a sense of responsibility and rest satisfied with the goal of utilizing atomic energy for peaceful purposes, so long does our thinking remain in midpassage, as it were. This half-heartedness will assure for all time, and thoroughly at that, that the world of technology will continue in its metaphysical preponderance.

However, who has decided that nature as such must for all future time remain nature as modern physics deals with it and history must present itself only as the object of academic historians? To be sure, we can neither repudiate the present-day world of technology as the work of the devil, nor may we nullify it in case it does not take care of this automatically.

Still less ought we to hanker after the opinion that the world of technology is such that it will simply prevent a liberating leap. Such an opinion, let it be noted, takes in a fit of obsession the actual for what alone is real. At all events, this opinion is phantastic. Quite different, however, the premeditation which looks anticipatingly to what is tending toward us invitingly as the identical essence of Man and Being.

Thought required more than two thousand years in order to comprehend fully such a simple relationship as that of mediation within identity. Are *we*, then, entitled to opine that the return of thought into the original essence of identity, can be accomplished in a day? It is precisely because this return demands a leap that it takes its own good time. The time is that of Thought which is different from that of calculating which in this day and age everywhere tugs at our thinking. Nowadays, the mechanical brain figures out in a second thousands of relations. But in spite of their technical usefulness such machines lack Being.

Whatever and however we may attempt to think, we will think in the context of tradition. Tradition preponderates if we are liberated from afterthinking[30] into anticipatory thinking which is no longer a planning.

Not until we turn our thoughts toward what has already been thought, shall we be employed for what has yet to be thought.

The Onto-theo-logical nature of Metaphysics

THE ONTO-THEO-LOGICAL
NATURE OF METAPHYSICS

In this seminar we made an attempt to engage Hegel in conversation. A conversation with a thinker can only deal with the object of thought. By "object" we mean, depending on the given situation, the case in dispute, the thing to be argued about which alone is for thought *the* case which concerns thought. However, strife over this thing which is in dispute was by no means started by thought without good reason, as it were. Object for thought is that which is the disputable proper in a strife. The word strife[31] means principally not discord but distress. The object of thought bothers thinking in such a manner as to lead thought first to its object and, thence, to itself.

For Hegel the object of thought is thought as such. In order not to misinterpret circumscribing the object under consideration, that is, thought as such, either psychologically or epistemologically, we are obliged to add by way of explanation: Thought as such, in the developed fullness of the suchness of what is thought. What we mean here by suchness of thought can only be understood through Kant, from the nature of the transcendental which Hegel, how-ever, thinks as absolute, which in turn means speculative to him. This is what Hegel had in mind when he spoke of the thinking of thought as such that it is developed "purely in the element of thought." [32] If we are to interpret this tersely and topically—which scarcely does justice in our thinking to the matter under consideration—we would have to say: The object of thinking for Hegel is "thought." However, unfolded to the depths of its essential freedom, this is "the absolute Idea." Hegel says of it toward the end of the *Science of Logic*[33]: "The absolute Idea alone is *Being,* imperishable *Life, Truth knowing itself,* and it is *Truth complete.*" Thus, Hegel himself bestows that name which is written over the whole object of occidental thinking, and he bestows it expressly on the object of his own thinking, the name of *Being.*

In the seminar[34] we discussed the severalfold and yet unified use of the word "Being." For Hegel, Being means, first of all, but *never exclusively,* "indefinite immediacy." Being is looked upon from the point of view of determining mediation, that is, from absolute notion and, hence, in relation to it. "The Truth of Being is Essence," [35] in other words, absolute reflection. The Truth of Essence is Notion in the sense of an in-finite knowing-itself. Being is absolute thought thinking itself. Absolute thought alone is the Truth of Being, it "is" Being. Truth, in Hegel, everywhere is equivalent to self-assured knowledge of what-may-be-known as such.

Hegel, however, thinks the object of his thinking topically at first in a conversation with the history of previous thinking. Hegel is the first one who can and must think in that way. Hegel's relationship to the history of philosophy is speculative and historic only in so far as it is speculative. The characteristic movement in history is an event in the sense of a dialectical process. Hegel writes:[36] "The same development of thought which is treated in the history of philosophy is being portrayed in every philosophy, yet emancipated from that historic externality, *purely in the element of thinking.*"

At this we are startled and stymied. Philosophy as such and the history of philosophy are, according to Hegel's own words, supposed to stand in relation of externality to each other. Yet, the externality of which Hegel thinks is by no means external in the sense of mere superficiality and indifference. Externality in this context refers to "outside of." "Outside" is where all history and every real process has its domicile as contrasted with the movement of the absolute Idea. The externality of history as explained in relation to the Idea is the result of the self-alienation of the Idea. Externality is itself a dialectical determination. We are, therefore, way off in our understanding of the real thought of Hegel's if we note as a fact that Hegel has welded into a unity historic conceptions and systematic thought in philosophy. For in Hegel's case it is neither a matter of an academic concept of history nor a system in the

37

sense of a theoretical structure.

What is on our mind as we make these remarks about philosophy and its relation to history? We intend to show that the object of thinking is, for Hegel, historical as such; but historical must be taken in the sense of a happening whose character as process is determined by the dialectic of Being. Object of thinking, for Hegel, is Being as self-thinking thought which ultimately becomes self-conscious in the process of its speculative development. Thus, thought runs through stages of various developments and, hence, must of necessity pass through previously undeveloped phases.

Thus there arises ultimately in Hegel's experience of the object of thinking a peculiar maxim, the authoritative way and manner in which he speaks to the thinkers preceding him.

Therefore, if we wish to attempt a conversation with Hegel's thought, we must talk to him not only about the same topic, but about the same topic in the same way. Nevertheless, the Same is not the identical. In identity difference disappears. In the Same difference appears. It appears the more urgently the more determinately we engage in thinking about the same object in the same manner. Hegel thinks of the Being of Existence speculative-historically. Now, in so far as Hegel's thinking belongs into a period of history (this does not by any stretch of the imagination mean to the past), we shall attempt to think about Hegel's Being in the same way, that is, historically.

Thinking can stay with a topic only by becoming more pertinent to the matter under consideration in the process of remaining-with-it, by having the same topic become more disputable. This being the case, the topic requires thought to put up with it in its idiosyncrasy, hold its ground by establishing a correspondence, and brings the matter to an issue. Thought, if it sticks to its topic, must, if the topic is Being, consent to an issue with Being. Accordingly, in our conversation with Hegel as well as in the interest of what has just been stated, we are obliged at the outset to clarify the sameness of the identical topic. In agreement with what we said it is incumbent on us to elucidate in our discourse with the history of philosophy the difference in the topic of thinking concomitantly with the difference in historical reality. In this lecture such a clarification has to be necessarily brief and sketchy.

For the purpose of shedding light on the disparity which obtains between Hegel's thinking and the thinking we shall attempt, let us consider three things.

Our questions are:

1. What is the object of thinking in his and in our case?

2. What is the criterion in a discourse involving

the history of thought in his and in our case?

3. What is the character of the discourse in his and in our case?

Concerning the First Question

For Hegel, the object of thought is Being in view of the suchness of existential thought in and as absolute Thought. For us, the object of thinking is the Same, hence, Being, but Being in view of its difference from Existence. Expressed even more precisely, for Hegel the object of thinking is Thought as absolute Notion. For us, the object of thinking is, by way of a first statement, difference *as* difference.[37]

Concerning the Second Question

For Hegel, the criterion for the discussion involving the history of philosophy is the degree of penetration into the vigor and milieu of that which was thought by former thinkers. It is not by chance that Hegel establishes his maxim in the course of his conversation with Spinoza and prior to a discussion with Kant.[38] In Spinoza Hegel discovers the perfect "point of view of substance," which, however, cannot be the highest because Being has not been thought of as yet to the degree and absolutely fundamentally as self-thinking Thought. Being, as substance and sub-stantiality, has not yet unfolded itself as subject in its absolute subjectivity. Nevertheless, Spinoza is stimulating the entire thinking of German idealism again and again and immediately generates a con-tradiction because he has Thought start with the Ab-solute. The way of Kant, on the contrary, is different and one that is by far more decisive for absolutistic idealistic thought and for philosophy in general than the system of Spinoza. Hegel sees in Kant's idea of the original synthesis of apperception "one of the profoundest principles for speculative develop-ment." [39] The relative influence of thinkers Hegel discovers in what they thought in so far as it may be raised to the appropriate stage of absolute Thought. Thought becomes absolute only by virtue of the fact that it moves in its dialectic-speculative process and requires for it an appropriate graduation.

For us, the criterion in our discussion involving historical tradition is the same in so far as it is a matter of penetrating the vigor of prior thinking. However, we are not looking for vigor in what has already been thought, but in something that has not yet been thought. It is in this something which pro-vides thought with the sphere in which it has its being. Still it is what has been thought that first pre-pares the way for the not-yet-thought which enters again and again with its overabundance. The standard for that which has not yet been thought does not lead to an incorporation of what has previously been

41

thought into a still higher development and systematization which outdistances it, but demands the release of traditional thinking into the past which is still preserved. Originally, the past controls tradition throughout and constitutes its anterior being without being thought of specially as and in terms of a beginning.

Concerning the Third Question

For Hegel, the discussion involving the previous history of philosophy has the character of a cancellation,[40] that is, of mediating understanding in the sense of finding absolute Reason.

For us, the character of the discussion involving the history of thought no longer signifies cancellation, but "backtracking." [41]

Cancellation leads to the high-level gathering realm of the absolutely posited truth in the sense of a perfectly unfolded certainty of self-knowing knowledge.

The "back track" reveals the realm thus far skipped on the basis of which the essence of truth becomes for the first time worthy to be thought.

After this brief characterization of the difference between Hegel's thinking and our own regarding the object, criterion, and character of a discussion involving the history of thought, we shall attempt to promote our discussion with Hegel, which we have already begun, a trifle more in the direction of clarity. By this we mean that we shall dare to make an attempt at "backtracking."

The phrase "backtracking" easily makes for several misinterpretations. To "backtrack" does not imply taking an isolated step in one's thinking, but a kind of thought movement, and a rather long way. In so far as "backtracking" determines the character of our discussion involving the history of occidental thought, thinking leads us, in a manner of speaking, out of what has up to now been thought in philosophy. Thought steps aside from its object, Being, and thus changes what is thought into the opposite wherein we glimpse it especially in view of what constitutes the source of all this thinking because basically it makes the realm of its abode available. This is, in contrast to Hegel, not a traditional, already posed problem, but it is the problem which has never even been asked throughout the history of thought. For the time being and unavoidably we designate it in the language of tradition. We speak of a *difference* between Being and Existence. The "back track" starts with what has not yet been thought, from difference as such, to proceed toward what is yet to be thought. That is the *oblivion* of difference. The oblivion we have in mind here is that of an enshrouding[42] of difference as such—we are thinking of a *Léthe* (concealment). This enshrouding originally went unnoticed. Oblivion belongs to difference because the latter belongs to the former. It is not as if oblivion overcame

43

subsequently difference in consequence of the forgetfulness of man's thinking.

The difference of Existence and Being is the realm within which metaphysics, that is, occidental thinking in the totality of its essence can be what in effect it is. "Backtracking" hence goes from metaphysics into the essence of metaphysics. The remark concerning Hegel's use of the severally interpreted main term "Being" permits us to recognize that any use of the word Being and Existence can never be fixed for *a particular* epoch of history during which clarity has been introduced into the concept "Being." Moreover, if we speak of "Being" we never take this word in the sense of a species under whose empty generality the doctrines concerning existence, historically considered, belong as individual cases. "Being," as the case may be, proclaims destiny and, hence, control of tradition.

Now, the "back track" from metaphysics into its essence requires, however, duration and endurance whose limits are known to us. Only one thing is clear: The "Back track" needs preparation which must be hazarded now and here. We do this, however, in view of Existence as such in the Whole, as it now *is* and begins to show itself more unambiguously as time goes on. What now *is* has been given the stamp by the domineering nature of modern technology. This hegemony has already found its expression in all areas of life in characteristics going by various names, such as functionalization, perfection, automatization, bureaucratization, information. Just as we call our concept of living reality biology, we could call the presentation and structuralizing of the thoroughly technically-permeated existence technology. This term may serve as a designation for the metaphysics of the atomic age. The "back track" from metaphysics into the essence of metaphysics is— seen as of now and based on insight into the present— the trek from technology, from the present age with its description and interpretation geared to technology, into the *essence* of modern technology which we will yet have to master in thought.

Let this suggestion also suffice to keep away the other natural misinterpretation of the term "back track," meaning the opinion that the trek consists in going back in history to the earliest thinkers of occidental philosophy. Of course, the whereto of the "back track" unfolds and becomes apparent only when the "backtracking" has been accomplished.

In order to obtain a comprehensive view of the Hegelian metaphysics[43] in our seminar, we chose expediently a discussion of the section with which the first book of the *Science of Logic,* "The Doctrine of Being," begins. Even the title of the section furnishes enough food for thought in every word. It says: "Wherewith must we start science?" Hegel's answer to this question consists in the demonstration that the beginning is of a "speculative nature." This means that the beginning is neither something immediate nor something mediate. The nature of this beginning we then endeavored to express in one speculative statement: "The beginning is the result." According to the plural interpretation of the dialectic, the "is" in this sentence indicates several things. For once, it conveys that the beginning is—taking the *resultare* literally[44]—the rebounding of thought reflecting upon itself from the perfection of dialectical movement. The perfection of this movement, the absolute Idea, is the unfolded closed Whole, the fullness of Being. The rebound from this fullness results in the emptiness of Being. Science (the absolute self-knowing knowledge) must begin here. Beginning and end of the movement, and prior to them the movement itself, remains everywhere Being. Being asserts itself as internally gyrating movement from fullness to extreme alienation and from alienation to self-perfecting fullness. Object of thought is, hence, for Hegel thought thinking itself as internally gyrating Being. Were we to reverse the speculative statement concerning the beginning, which is not only justifiable but necessary, it would read: "The result is the beginning." Actually, we ought to start with the result in so far as the beginning evolves from it.

This says the same as does the remark which Hegel inserts casually and parenthetically in the section dealing with the Beginning, toward the end:[45] ". . . (and it would seem *God* has the indisputable right that we should begin with him)." According to the problem stated in the section-heading we are

46

concerned with the "beginning of science." If science has to start with God, then it is the science of God, theology. This designation suggests its later significance. Accordingly, theo-logy is a statement made by representational thinking about God. *Theólogos, theología,* means, first and foremost, the mythico-poetical legendizing about gods without any connection with a doctrine of faith or a church doctrine.

Why is "science"—since Fichte the name for metaphysics—why is science theology? I reply, because science is the systematic development of knowledge, in which form the Being of Existence knows itself and thus is true. The scholastic title for the Science of Being, that is, the Science of Existence as such in general, as it emerged during the transition period from the Middle Ages to the present era, is ontosophy or ontology.

Now, occidental metaphysics, however, has been since its beginnings among the Greeks and still is uncommitted to these labels, especially those of ontology and theology. In my inaugural lecture *What is Metaphysics?* (1929) I, therefore, clarified metaphysics as a problem of Existence as such *and* Existence in the Whole. The totality of the Whole is the unity of Existence, which unity unites by virtue of being the productive ground. For him who can read this means that metaphysics is onto-theo-logic. Whoever has, through his own development, experienced theology, be it that of Christian faith, or that of philosophy, will prefer nowadays to be silent about God as an object of thought and thinking. For, the onto-theological character of metaphysics has become questionable to thinking persons, not by reason of some sort of atheism, but because of an intellectual experience in which the still *unthought* unity of the essence of metaphysics revealed itself within onto-theo-logic. However, the essence of this metaphysics will still remain to our minds as what is most worthy of giving thought to so long as thought does not break off arbitrarily and hence unappropriately the discussion involving its fateful tradition.

In the 5th edition of *What is Metaphysics?* (1949) I made special reference in the supplemental Introduction to the onto-theological essence of metaphysics.[46] However, it would be rash to assert that metaphysics is theology because it is reputed to be ontology. We should begin by saying that metaphysics is theology, a statement about God, because God enters philosophy. In this way the problem becomes more acute as a problem regarding the onto-theo-logical character of metaphysics: How does God get into philosophy, not only into recent philosophy, but into philosophy as such? This problem can be answered only if, as a problem, it has previously been sufficiently developed.

The problem as to how God got into philosophy can only then be thought through and done justice to, if in the course of investigation the whither of God has become sufficiently clear. It is the problem of philosophy as such. So long as we scan the history of philosophy merely historically we shall find that God got everywhere into it. Let us suppose, however, that philosophy, as thought, is the free, spontaneously pursued involvement in Existence as such, then God can get into philosophy only in so far as philosophy as such autonomously and by virtue of its own essence demands it and lays down the that and the how of God entering her. The problem as to how God gets into philosophy, therefore, reverts to the problem: Whence comes the essential onto-theological constitution of metaphysics? Taking on the problem thus formulated means, however, that we are "backtracking."

In doing this we now give serious thought to the original essence of the onto-theological structure of all metaphysics and ask the question: How does God get into metaphysics and along with him and correspondingly, theology and its onto-theological character? We are putting this question in a discussion involving the whole of the history of philosophy. At the same time, however, we ask with a special side glance toward Hegel, an occasion for us to first turn to something peculiar.

Hegel is thinking Being in its most complete emptiness, thus in terms the most universal. At the same time he thinks Being in its most perfect fullness. Nevertheless, he does not call speculative philosophy, i.e., philosophy proper, onto-theology, but "Science of Logic." With this terminology Hegel brings something decisive to the fore. One could, of course, immediately explain why metaphysics is called "logic" by pointing out that, for Hegel, the object of thought is "Thought," taking the word *singulare tantum,* in the singular plain and simple. Thought, thinking, is, as everyone knows and according to ancient practice considered the theme of logic. That much is certain. But it is just as incontrovertibly established that Hegel, true to tradition, discovers the object of thought in Existence as such and in the Whole, that is, in the movement of Being from emptiness to developed fullness.

Now, how is it possible that "Being" will undertake at all to represent itself as "thought"? How otherwise can it do it than by virtue of the fact that Being, as ground, is already impressed, while thinking —because it belongs together with Being—collects on Being as the ground, to fathom and understand it. Being manifests itself as thought which means that the Being of Existence reveals itself as self-fathoming and self-justifying ground. Ground and *ratio* (reason) are in their original essence the *lógos* in the sense of the collective problematic,[47] the *'En Pánta.* Thus, "science," i.e., metaphysics, is for Hegel "logic" not really because science has thought for its object, but because the object of thought remains *Being.* Being, however, privately engages thought for the purpose of understanding, and it has done so since the early stages of unmasking itself in the imprint of the *Lógos,* which is the authenticating reason.[48]

Metaphysics thinks Existence as such, in general. Metaphysics thinks Existence as such, that is, in the Whole. Metaphysics thinks the Being of Existence in the fathoming unity of the greatest generality, that is, the universal equi-valence, as well as in the understanding unity of totality, which is highest above all else. Thus, we presuppose the Being of Existence as authenticating reason. Hence, all metaphysics is, basically, the fathoming from the very bottom, reasoning which renders account of the ground, replies, and finally calls it to account.

Why should we mention this at all? Because we want to experience the stereotyped terms ontology, theology, and onto-theology in their core. At the start, however, and ordinarily, the terms ontology and theology strike us just like other well-known terms, such as psychology, biology, cosmology, archeology. The final syllable, —[o]logy, quite generally and readily suggests that we are dealing with the sciences of the soul, of living reality, of the cosmos, and of antiquities. Yet, in -ology there lies concealed not only the logical in the sense of the consistent and declaratory in general, which articulates, promotes, safeguards and communicates all scientific knowledge. The -logia is in every case the totality of a reticulated system of understandings wherein the objects of science are thought with a view to their rational basis, will say, are understood. Ontology and theology, by contrast, are "logia" in so far as they fathom Existence as such and seek its ground in the Whole. They render account of Being as the ground of the Existent. They are answerable to the *Lógos* and are, in quite an essential sense, conforming to the *Lógos,* that is, the logic of the *Lógos.* Accordingly, they should be called more properly onto-logic and theo-logic. More appropriately and more descriptively metaphysics should be thought of as onto-theo-logic.

Now we understand the term "logic" in essentially the sense which includes also the designation used by Hegel and first really explains it. Logic is, to be sure, the name for that particular thinking which everywhere tries to fathom and comprehend Existence as such within the totality of Being as ground (*Lógos*). The basic character of metaphysics is onto-theo-logic. Thus we are enabled to explain how God gets into philosophy.

To what extent are we successful with our explanation? Well, in so far as we take notice that the object of thought is Existence as such, that is, Being, which reveals itself in the essential nature of the ground. In accordance, the object of thought, Being as ground, is thought through thoroughly only when we have before our mental eye the idea of the ground as a primary ground, *prōtē 'arché.* The original object of thought presents itself as the proto-object, the *causa prima* (first Cause) which corresponds in reasoning to the regress to the *ultima ratio* (Ultimate Reason), the final account. The Being of Existence in the sense of the ground is represented fully only as *causa sui*. But in these words we have touched upon the metaphysical concept of God. Metaphysics is obliged to think in the direction of God because the cause of thought is Being, while Being is ground in a variety of ways: as *Lógos,* as *Hypokeímenon,* as Substance, as Subject.

This explanation presumably touches upon something that is correct. Still, it remains absolutely insufficient for an investigation of the essence of metaphysics. For, metaphysics is not only theo-logic, but also onto-logic. Metaphysics, above all, is not only one and/or the other. Rather, metaphysics is theo-logic because it is onto-logic. It is this because it is that. The essential onto-theological constitution of metaphysics cannot be explained either on the basis of theologic nor on that of ontologic, provided an explanation will ever suffice for what we still have to reflect on.

Let it be noted that we have not yet given thought to the problem as to the type of unity in which ontologic and theologic belong together, nor have we considered the origin of this unity, nor the difference of the differentia which unite ontologic and theologic. For, apparently, we are concerned not with bringing together two independently existing disciplines of metaphysics, but with the unity of *what* in ontologic and theologic is the object of enquiry and thought. *That* is Existence as such in the universal and primary *at one with* the Existent as such in the Highest and Ultimate. The unity of the One is such that the Ultimate understands the First in its own way and the First the Ultimate in its own way. The difference in both ways of understanding is part of the difference we have mentioned but not yet thought about.

It is in the unity of Existence as such in the most Universal and in the Highest that we find rests the essential constitution of metaphysics.

First of all we are obliged to discuss the problem of the onto-theological nature of metaphysics problematically pure and simple. Only the object of thought itself can usher us into the realm which is discussed in the problem as to the onto-theological constitution of metaphysics. We can accomplish this by thinking more objectively about the object of thought. The object of thought is traditionally known in occidental thinking by the name this object[49] just a trifle more objectively, should we pay more careful attention to the debatable in the object, then we should see that always and everywhere *Being* means the Being of *Existence*, in which phrase the possessive case is to be thought as a genitivus subjectivus. Of course, we speak with reservations about a possessive case as applied to object and subject, for these labels, subject and object, have on their part arisen from an imprint of Being. The only thing that is clear is that in the case of the Being of Existence and the Existence and the Existence of Being we are concerned every time with a difference.

We think of Being, therefore, as object only when

we think it as different from Existence and think Existence as different from Being. Thus, difference proper emerges. If we attempt to form an image of it, we shall discover that we are immediately tempted to comprehend difference as a relation which our thinking has added to Being and to Existence. As a result, difference is reduced to a distinction, to a product of human intelligence.

However, let us assume for once that difference is an addition of our forming a mental image, then the problem arises: An addition to what? And the answer we get is: to Existence. Well and good. But what do we mean by this "Existence"? What else do we mean by it than such as is? Thus we accommodate the alleged addition, the idea of a difference, under Being. Yet, "Being" itself proclaims: Being which is *Existence*. Wherever we would introduce difference as an alleged addition, we always meet Existence and Being in their difference. It is as in Grimm's fairy tale of the rabbit and the hedgehog: "I's all here." Now, we could treat this odd state of affairs that Existence and Being, each in its own way, are to be discovered through and in difference, in a pompous fashion and explain it as follows. "It cannot be helped that our representational thinking is so organized and constituted that prior to any operation it establishes difference everywhere between Existence and Being, above one's head, as it were, and again in one's head where it seems to originate." Much could be said anent this apparently natural yet all too ready explanation. Still more problems could be posed, above all this. Where do we get this "between" from in which difference is, as it were, to be intercalated?

Let us be done now with opinions and explanations. Instead let us make the following observation. What we call difference we find everywhere and at all times in the object of thought, in Existence as such, and we come up against it in a manner so free of doubt that we do not pay any particular attention to it. Nothing moreover, seems to compel us to take particular notice. We are at liberty in our thinking not to give any thought to difference or to reflect on it specifically. Yet, this liberty does not hold for all cases. By chance it may occur that thought will find itself called upon to answer the question: What is the meaning of this oft-mentioned Being? If under these conditions Being exhibits itself as a being of . . ., in the genitive of difference, then the question just asked would be more to the point if rephrased: What in your opinion is difference if both Being as well as Existence each in their own way appear *through difference*? In order to do justice to this question we must first of all maneuver ourselves into an objective opposition to difference. This opposition appears when we "backtrack." For it is only through the dis-tance brought about by "backtracking" that the close-by as such presents itself, that proximity appears for the first time. In "backtracking" we release the object of thought, Being as difference, into its

56

opposite. The opposite may remain absolutely objectless.

Still with an eye to difference, yet releasing it in "backtracking" into that which is *to*-be-thought[50] we can assert the following. Being of Existence means the type of Being which Existence is. The "is" in this case is to be taken transitively, as implying passage. Being asserts its nature[51] here in the manner of a transition to Existence. However, Being does not go over toward or into Existence by leaving its place or position, as if Existence, previously devoid of Being, could be contacted by Being for the first time. Being transcends and covers, while revealing itself, what is encountered in open presence by such enthrallment. Encounter means seeking refuge in open presence, thus, being in sheltered presence, being an Existent.[52]

Being exhibits itself as revealing enthrallment. Existence as such manifests itself as an encounter fleeing into unmasked presence.

Being in the sense of revealing enthrallment and Existence as such in the sense of refuge-seeking encounter have their being as elements that have been differentiated from the Same, that which underlies difference.[53] What underlies distinction is what originally is responsible for yielding and keeping apart the between, wherein enthrallment and encounter are conjoined and mutually supported in their fluctuating relationships. The difference of Being and

57

Existence as the ground of distinction between enthrallment and encounter lies in the *unmasking-en-
shrouding issue* of both. Light is shed throughout the
issue on the self-enshrouding occlusion. It is this pervading luminosity which is responsible for the re-
ciprocity of enthrallment and encounter.

In our attempt to reflect on difference as such we
do not cause its disappearance but we are following
it through to its essential origin. *En route* there we
had to give thought to the issue between enthrallment and encounter. What is at stake is really the
object of thought more objectively considered in the
"backtracking." In other words, it is Being thought
of as emerging from difference.

To be sure, at this point we have to intersperse a
remark which has to do with our speaking of the object of thought and will engage our attention again
and again. Supposing we mention "Being," then we
are using the word in the widest possible and most
indeterminate generality. Even when speaking only
of a generality, have we thought of Being in an in-
appropriate manner. We visualize Being in a way
in which It (Being) never presents itself. The manner in which the object of thought, that is, Being,
behaves remains unique. The habitual mode of
thought can forever enlighten us about this unique
situation only insufficiently in the beginning. Let
us illustrate this by an example. From the outset we
should be aware of the fact, however, that nowhere
in Existence is there an example of the essence of

Being, presumably because the essence of Being is the play itself.

In order to characterize the universality of the general, Hegel at one time gave the following illustration: Someone wanted to buy fruit in a store. He asked for fruit. They gave him apples, pears, they handed him peaches, cherries, grapes. But the customer rejected what was offered him. He wanted fruit, and wanted it at any cost. Now, what was offered him *was*, indeed, every time fruit. Nevertheless, we come to the conclusion that fruit cannot be bought.

Impossible to the nth degree would be imagining "Being" as the universal belonging to every case of Existence. Being we meet only occasionally in this or that fate-enmeshed formulation: *Phýsis, Lógos, 'En, Idéa, Enérgeia,* substantiality, objectivity, subjectivity, Will, Will to Power, Will to Will. But such examples from the fateful history of man we shall not find neatly arranged like apples, pears, and peaches, displayed on the counter of historical ideas.

Nevertheless, didn't we learn of Being in the historic order and sequence of the dialectical process which Hegel thought? Certainly. But in this case too Being reveals itself only in the light in which it made itself manifest for Hegel. By this we mean that the manner in which Being presents itself must assuredly be determined by the manner in which it manifests itself. The peculiar manner, however, is the impress of destiny, the stamp of the prevailing epoch which as such assumes being for us only to the extent to which we permit it to rejoin what it properly has been. It is only in the sudden impact of a moment of remembrance that we gain access to destiny. This is likewise true in the experience of a special modal difference between Being and Existence to which an individual interpretation of Existence as such corresponds. What has been stated is true above all also for our attempt to think of difference as the issue between revealing enthrallment and enshrouding encounter as we are "backtracking" from forgetfulness of difference as such. To be sure, as we are listening more attentively we receive documentation of the fact that in the verbal formulation of this we have already permitted the past to speak its piece in as much as we are thinking of revealing and enshrouding, of passage (transcendence) and of encounter (presence). By pursuing this discussion of the difference of Being and Existence into the issue as a preliminary to its essence, it is perhaps possible that something diffusive comes to the fore which pervades the destiny of Being from its beginning to its consummation. Nevertheless, it is still difficult to describe how we are to think of this pervasiveness when it is neither a universal valid for all cases, nor a law which assures the necessity of a process in the dialectic sense.

What we are now primarily concerned with in our undertaking is gaining an insight into the possibility of thinking of difference as an issue which is to clarify in how far the onto-theological constitution of meta-physics derives its original essence from the issue which we meet at the beginning of the history of metaphysics, runs through its periods and yet remains everywhere hidden, and hence forgotten, *as* the issue in an oblivion which escapes even us.

In order to facilitate the insight mentioned above, let us reflect on Being, and within it on difference, and within difference on the issue from the point of view of that cast of Being through which Being became exposed as *Lógos*, or, Reason. Being manifests itself in revealing enthrallment by letting the encountering reality remain problematic, by authentication in the manifold methods of assembling and discovering. Existence, as such—the encounter seeking refuge in overtness—is what is authenticated. That which is authenticated and consequently effected, then authenticates in its own way, to be sure, by effecting, will say, causing. The issue between fathoming and authentication as such not only keeps both apart, it keeps them also in a state of togetherness. The points at issue are so interlaced in the issue that not only Being as ground authenticates Existence, but Existence, in turn, and by its own methods, authenticates Being, that is, causes it. Such, Existence can accomplish only in so far as it "is" the fullness of Being or, in other words, as Existence *par excellence*.

At this point our reflection carries us into an exciting nexus. Being has its essence in *Lógos*, in the sense of Reason, of the problematic. Thought of collectively, the same *Lógos* is the unifying agent, the *'En*. However, this *'En* is twofold. For once, it is the Unifying One in the sense of the ubiquitous First and, hence, the Most Universal; at the same time it is the One Unifying One in the sense of the Highest (Zeus). *Lógos,* by virtue of finding reasons, gathers everything into the universal and by understanding gathers everything from the Unique. That, moreover, the same *Lógos* harbors within itself the essential origin of linguistic formulation and thus determines the mode of speaking as logical in the widest sense, may only be mentioned by the way.

In so far as Being has its essence in the Being of Existence, in difference, in an issue, do authentication and understanding in their joining issues and dropping them continue, does Being authenticate Existence, does Existence fathom Being as Existence *par excellence*. The One enthralls the Other, the One is encountered in the Other. Enthrallment and encounter appear alternatingly one in the other in reflection. Speaking from the point of view of difference this means that the issue is a circling, a revolving, one around the other, of Being and Existence. The act of authentication itself appears within the clearing of the issue as something which *is,* hence on its own initiative demands, as Existence, the corresponding understanding by something existing. This something is causation, a causation, to be sure, by the highest Cause.

One of the classical proofs for this fact in the history of metaphysics may be found in a text of Leibniz's which has hardly been noticed, a text which we tersely describe as "The 24 Theses of Metaphysics." [54]

Metaphysics corresponds to Being as *Lógos* and is, accordingly, in its main feature at all events logic. But it is a logic which thinks the Being of Existence; therefore, it is the logic which is determined by the different: It is onto-theo-logic.

In so far as metaphysics thinks Existence as such in terms of the Whole, it visualizes Existence from the point of view of the different in the difference without paying attention to difference as difference.

The different exhibits itself as the Being of Existence in the Universal and as the Being of Existence in the Highest.

Because Being appears as the ground,[55] Existence is that which is authenticated. However, Existence *par excellence* is that which understands[56] in the sense of being the First Cause. If metaphysics thinks Existence with an eye toward its basis which is common to every individual Existent as such, then metaphysics is logic in the form of onto-logic. If metaphysics thinks Existence as such in terms of the Whole, that is, with an eye toward the highest all-understanding Existence, then metaphysics becomes logic in the form of theo-logic.

Because metaphysical thinking remains imbedded in difference which as such is not the object of thought, metaphysics is at one and the same time uniquely ontology and theology by virtue of the unifying oneness of the issue.

The onto-theological constitution of metaphysics hails from the pervasive influence of difference which joins and separates as ground and Existence, both authenticating and understanding, and is sustained by the issue in carrying the action through.

These novel terms which we have been using are meant to guide our thinking into realms which to designate the common terms of metaphysics, Being and Existence, ground-grounded, no longer suffice. For whatever these terms designate, whatever is represented by the mode of thinking stimulated by them, stems from difference as that which is different; their origin may no longer be included in the purview to metaphysics.

Insight into the onto-theological constitution of metaphysics shows a possible way of answering the question as to how God entered philosophy by going to the essence of metaphysics.

God entered philosophy through the issue which we think first of all as being the advance point in the essence of the difference between Being and Existence. Difference represents the ground plan in the essential structure of metaphysics. The issue yields and cedes Being as the pro-duc-tive ground, which ground in itself requires an appropriate understanding on the part of what it helped found. The appropriate understanding is equivalent to causation by the ultimate and original reality. This is the Cause as *causa sui,* and this is the just and proper name for God in philosophy. Man may neither pray to this God, nor may be sacrifice to him. Confronted by *causa sui* man may neither sink onto his knees nor could he sing and dance.

Accordingly, this thinking-less-God which must abandon the God of philosophy, God as *causa sui,* is, perhaps, closer to God the divinity. In our context this means merely that thinking-less-God is less restricted in dealing with him than onto-theo-logic would acknowledge.

With this remark we may have shed a little light on the path on which we find the type of thinking which is "backtracking" from metaphysics into the essence of metaphysics, from oblivion of difference as such into a fateful concealment of the issue which we no longer understand.

Nobody can possibly know whether, when, where and how this step thought is taking will open up into a true (event-bound) path, and lead to a passage and road construction. It could be that the sway of metaphysics will consolidate sooner than expected. We are thinking of the rise of modern technology and its developments, swift and limitless to the eye. It could also be that everything that is taking place while "backtracking" will only be utilized and incorporated in a continuing metaphysics in ways appropriate to itself and as the result of imaginative thinking.

In such a case the "back track" itself would not be

accomplished and the path which has been opened up and pointed out would not be used.

Easily such reflections impinge upon our minds, but they have no weight in relation to a difficulty of quite a different nature which we have to negotiate in "backtracking."

The difficulty is one of language. Our western languages are languages variously suited to metaphysical thinking. Whether the nature of western languages bears only the stamp of metaphysics and, hence, ultimately, that of onto-theo-logic, or whether these languages offer other possibilities of expressing and at the same time saying without expressing, must remain an open question. During the exercises in our seminar often enough difficulties arose to which verbal expression of thought was exposed. The little word "is" which is met everywhere in our language and tells of Being even where it does not come to the fore, harbors the entire fate of Being, from the *éstin gar einai* of Parmenides to the "is" of the speculative principle of Hegel and still further to the dissolution of the "is" in the positing of a will to power by Nietzsche.

A look into the difficulties originating in language should save us from prematurely recasting the language in which our present attempts in thinking have been couched. It should caution us to speak of an issue in the offing on the morrow instead of devoting all our efforts to thinking what we have formulated in language all the way through. For what we did say was said in a seminar. A seminar is, as the word indicates, a place and an occasion for disseminating here and there a grain, a seed of reflection which sometime or other will germinate as it may and bear fruit.

Notes

NOTES

(The notes are Heidegger's unless stated otherwise and
contain largely references to his own writings).

1. An attempt to think the thing may be consulted in
Vorträge und Aufsätze (Neske, Pfullingen, 1954), pp. 163-
181. The lecture *"Das Ding"* ("The Thing") was first
delivered within a series of lectures entitled *"Einblick in
das, was ist"* (A Look into What Is") in December, 1949,
at Bremen, and in the spring of 1950 at Bühlerhöhe.

2. *Das Ereignis.* Translator.

3. *Der Austrag.* Trl.

4. *And so does the English.* Trl.

5. Cf. the work referred to in note 1, pp. 231-256, for
an interpretation of this Parmenides fragment.

6. The German is *übereignet*, which could also be
translated by "assigned," "allotted." Trl.

7. Or, concerns Man. Both meanings are contained in
the German word *angeht*, or, as Heidegger writes it,
an-geht. Trl.

8. The German has, pregnantly, *An-wesen.* Trl.

9. In the somewhat stronger sense of "returned to."
Trl.

10. The German word is *Einkehr* which means putting
up as at an inn. Trl.

11. The original has *Sichabsetzen.* Trl.

12. *Sprung,* in German. Trl.

13. *Grund.* Trl.

14. The German word is *gründet.* Trl.

15. *Wohin wir schon eingelassen sind* may also be translated as "to where we have already entry." Trl.

16. We have here a play upon the word which is hyphenated: *an-wesen.* Trl.

17. The original has *die Konstellation beider.* Trl.

18. Cf. the work mentioned in note 1, pp. 13-70, regarding the essence of modern technology and present-day science.

19. We use the word hyphenated in order to imitate the German *Ge-stell,* which might also be translated as "con-texture." Trl.

20. German: *stellen.* Trl.

21. The word is derived from Latin *statuere,* to set, and hence is apposite to the German word *Gesetz,* or *Ge-setz,* as Heidegger writes it here. Trl.

22. These and other hyphenations are in imitation of Heidegger's practice. Trl.

23. This last phrase is interpretative. Trl.

24. In German: *hören.* Trl.

25. German: *Vereignen.* Trl.

26. German: *Zueignen.* The original for what we translate in the following sentence by concinnity is *Eignen.* Trl.

27. Event would be the usual translation of *Ereignis.* In view of what follows, and paralleling the German, we have chosen "concern" in the sense in which it is also listed in Webster: "That which relates or belongs to one." "Concern" is derived from *con* and *cerno* in Latin. One meaning of *cerno* is to "distinguish," "see," and, hence, has an etymology similar to *Ereignis* which comes from

OHG *ougen* and Gothic *augjan*, to show, which are derivatives from *Auge*, eye. By adopting and adapting "concern" to *Ereignis* we can now proceed with Heidegger's discussion which is an etymologizing around the concept *er-eignen* which originally derived from visual activity but now serves to convey the idea of happening, not without the overtones of reference to self and possession. Trl.

28. It will be necessary to call attention to the fact that the English "concern" has these same overtones as *Ereignis*. Trl.

29. We are attempting to imitate in translation the play upon the word *Satz* which means both principle and leap. Trl.

30. Or, reflection. Trl.

31. Etymologically related to "to stride" and "strive" in English and *Streit* in German, which Heidegger uses. Trl.

32. In paragraph 14 of the Introduction to the *Enzyklopädie*.

33. In G. Lasson's edition, vo. II, p. 484.

34. This whole paragraph is put parenthetically in the original. Trl.

35. *Die Wahrheit des Seins ist das Wesen.* Trl.

36. In the 14th paragraph of the *Enzyklopädie*.

37. For a detailed discussion of difference, cf. *Was heisst denken?* (Niemeyer, Tübingen, 1954) and *Zur Seinsfrage* (Klostermann, Frankfurt a.M., 1956).

38. *Science of Logic*, 3rd vol., *ed.* Lasson, vol. II, p. 216 ff.

39. *Ibid.*, p. 227.

40. For this and the subsequent discussion the reader is referred to Hegel as interpreted by William T. Harris

in his out-of-print works *Hegel's Doctrone of Reflection* (New York, 1881) and *Hegel's Logic* (Chicago, 1890), or Wanda Orynski: *Hegel Highlights: An Annotated Selection* (Philosophical Library, 1960). Trl.

41. The German is *der Schritt zurück*. Trl.

42. *Verhüllung*. Trl.

43. For an interpretation of Hegel's metaphysics, cf. *Holzwege* (Klostermann, Frankfurt a.M., 1950), pp. 105-192.

44. The reference is to the "result" in the just quoted sentence: "The beginning is the result." Trl.

45. Lasson, *op. cit.*, vol. I, p. 63.

46. P. 17 f. (7th *ed.*, p. 18 f.).

47. *Versammelndes Vorliegenlassen*. Trl.

48. *Der gründende Grund*. Trl.

49. *Brief über den Humanismus* (1947. *A Letter on Humanism*) which is only suggestive throughout, may be taken to stimulate the discussion of the object of thought, but not before going back in thought over what has been written here and in the other publications mentioned throughout the notes.

50. If the italicization should not sufficiently convey Heidegger's meaning in *das zu-Denkende*, we add that he wishes to bring out the idea of addition or supplementation. Trl.

51. The German has *west* which is related to the concept of to be as well as to become. Trl.

52. The end of this paragraph is less open to logical and intellectual penetration than mystical appreciation. This is true for the original and is not disclaimed for the translation. Trl.

53. It is quite impossible to render *Unter-shied* as difference here and yet retain Heidegger's meaning, hence

74

the paraphrase. Consequently, what follows is also not translation but paraphrase. Trl.

54. C. J. Gerhardt, *Die Philosophischen Schriften von G. W. Leibniz*, vol. VII, p. 289 ff. Cf. also *Der Satz vom Grund* (1957), p. 51 f.

55. Concerning Being as ground or reason, cf. the work mentioned in note 1, pp. 207-229, and *Der Satz vom Grund* (Neske, Pfullingen, 1957).

56. Here as elsewhere when "to understand" is used for *begründen*, the reader should take it literally as a "standing under," furnishing the ground, and thus not only recall the Anglo-Saxon meaning, but get the feel of Heidegger's allusion. Trl.

Glossary

GLOSSARY

absetzen, sich — to keep aloof
Allgemeine, das — general, universal
Allgemeinheit, die — universality
angehen (an-gehen) — to draw near; concern
ankommen — to encounter
Ankunft, die — arrival; encounter
ansprechen — to make a claim, demand
Anspruch, der — claim
anwesen (an-wesen) — to be present to, confront
Anwesen (An-wesen), das — being present, presence
Austrag, der — argument; issue
austragen — to bring to an issue

bergen — to shelter; obscure
bergen, sich — to seek refuge; enshroud
begründen — to understand, seek basic reasons
Begründung, die — understanding

Durchgängige, das — pervasive, pervading

eigentlich — authentic, genuine
eigentlicher — more genuine(ly)
Eignen, das — concinnity
Einkehr, die — return, homing
einkehren — to enter into, resort to

entbergen — to unmask
Entbergung, die — unmasking
enteignen — to alienate
ereignen — to concern
Ereignen, das — concern, solicitude
Ereignis (Er-eignis), das — concern
ergründen — to fathom

geborgen — existing in sheltered presence
Gedachtheit des Gedankens, die — suchness of thought
geeignet (ge-eignet) — concinnate
Gemächte, das — work, product
Gepräge, das — imprint
Geschick, das — destiny
geschicklich — what is destined, fate-enmeshed
Geschickliche, das — destiny
Gesetz (Ge-setz), das — law, statute
Gestell (Ge-stell), das — framework contexture
gestellt — framed
Gleiche, das — identical, same
Gleichheit, die — equality
Grund, der — ground; reason; authentication
gründen — to base; find or seek reasons; authenticate

Haltung, die — attitude

Konstellation, die — pattern

lichten, sich — to expose, become exposed
Lichtung, die — clearing

Massgabe, die — criterion

Ontologik, die — ontologic

80

Onto-Theologie, die — ontotheology
Onto-Theo-Logik, die — ontotheologic

prägen — to imprint, impress
Prägung, die — impress, stamp, imprint, cast; formulation

Sache des Denkens, die — object of thought, topic
sachlich — topical(ly); causal(ly)
Satz, der — principle; positing; advance, leap
Schritt zurück, der — back track
Sein, das — Being
Seiende, das — Existence
Seiendes, ein — Existent
Seiendste, das — Existence *par excellence*
Selbe, das — Same
Selbigkeit, die — state of being oneself, self-identity
Sichabsetzen, das — keeping aloof
Sichstellen, das — fronting; confrontation
Sprung, der — leap
stellen — to frame

Theologik (Theo-Logik), die — theologic

übereignen — to assign, allocate, allot
Uebergang, der — passage, transcendence
Ueberkommnis, die — enthrallment
Unverborgenheit, die — open presence, overtness

Verbergung, die — concealment
Vereignen, das — alienation
vereignet — alienated
vergeben — to dispense
Vergessenheit, die — oblivion
Verhüllung, die — enshrouding

verwinden — to implicate, convolute
Verwindung, die — implication

wesen — to be, assert being
Wesen, das — being; essence, nature
Wesensherkunft, die — original essence

Zueignen, das — dedication
zugeeignet — dedicated
Zuspruch, der — invitation